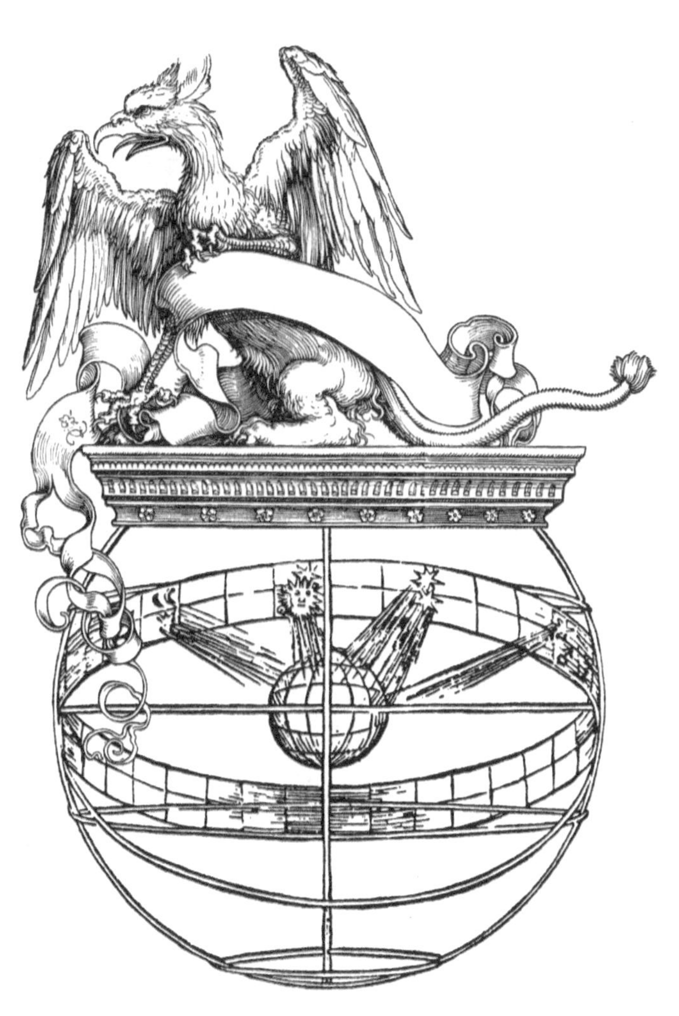

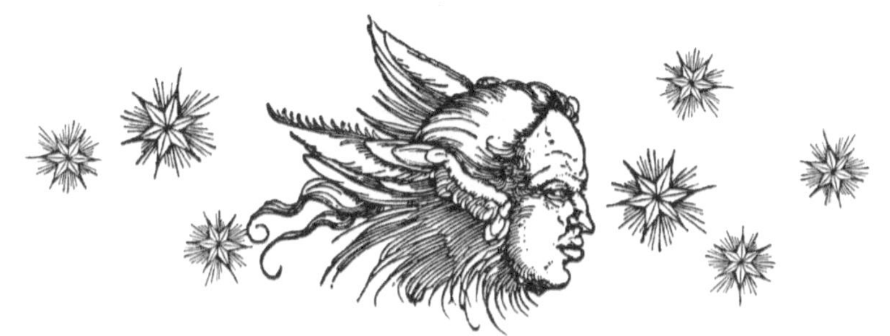

D·R·E·A·M·T·I·M·E

A Coloring Book by

Stephen Barnwell

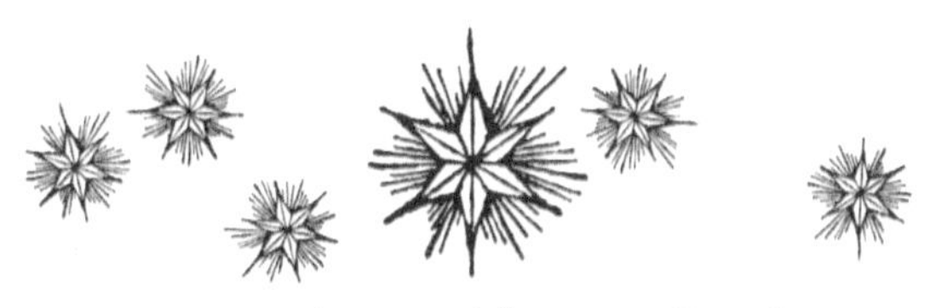

Antarctica Arts

DREAMTIME
Published by Antarctica Arts
GPO Box 7586, NY, NY 10116
books@AntarcticaArts.com
www.AntarcticaArts.com

DREAMTIME is a coloring book adaptation of *Oneirognosis, The Art of Dreaming* by Stephen Barnwell (Antarctica Arts, 2015, ISBN 9780991321612). Learn the art of dream-seeding, where you ask your dreams questions and receive answers.

ISBN Number 978-0-9913216-5-0

Printed by Amazon

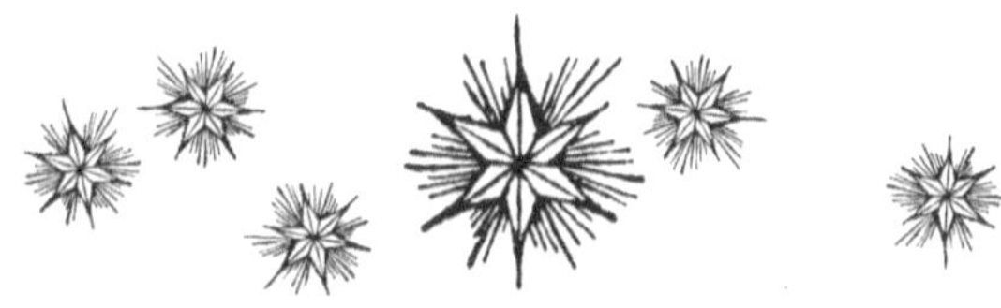

Where Dreams Happen

I

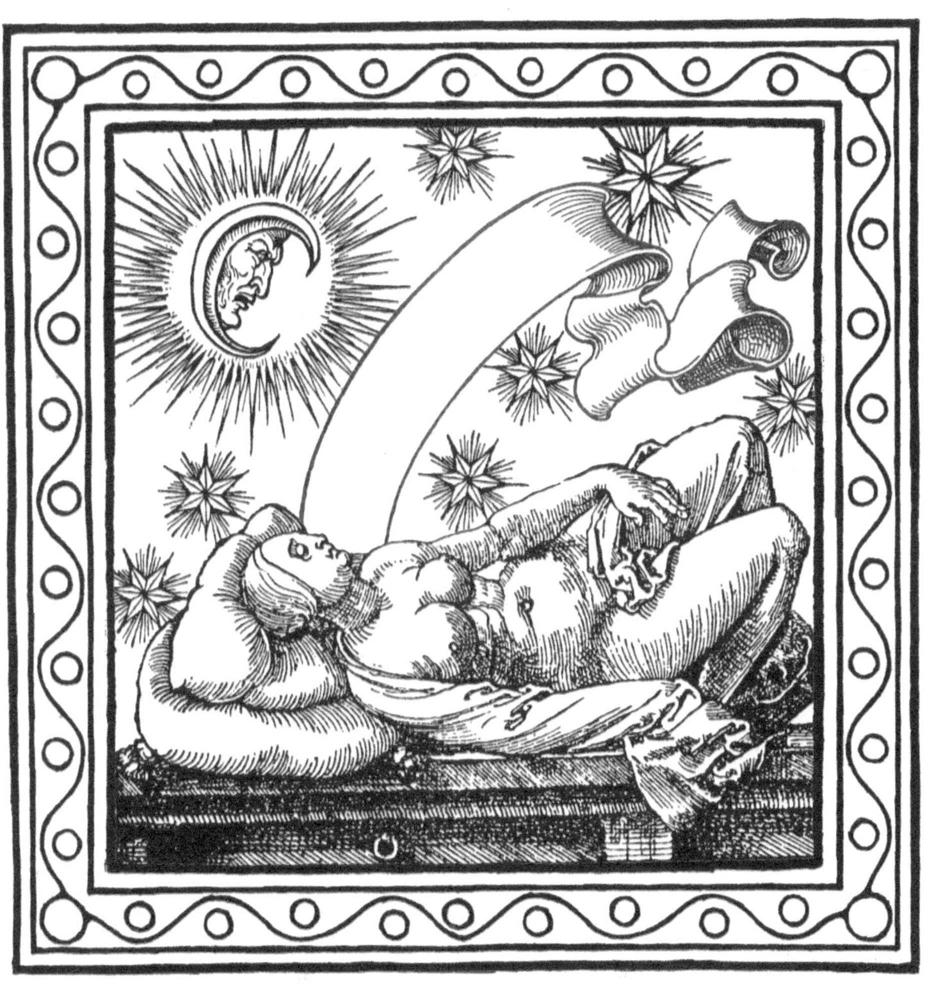

When we shift our gaze in sleep, a doorway into another reality is suddenly opened. Beyond it is a world just as real as our waking life, yet seen through clouded eyes.

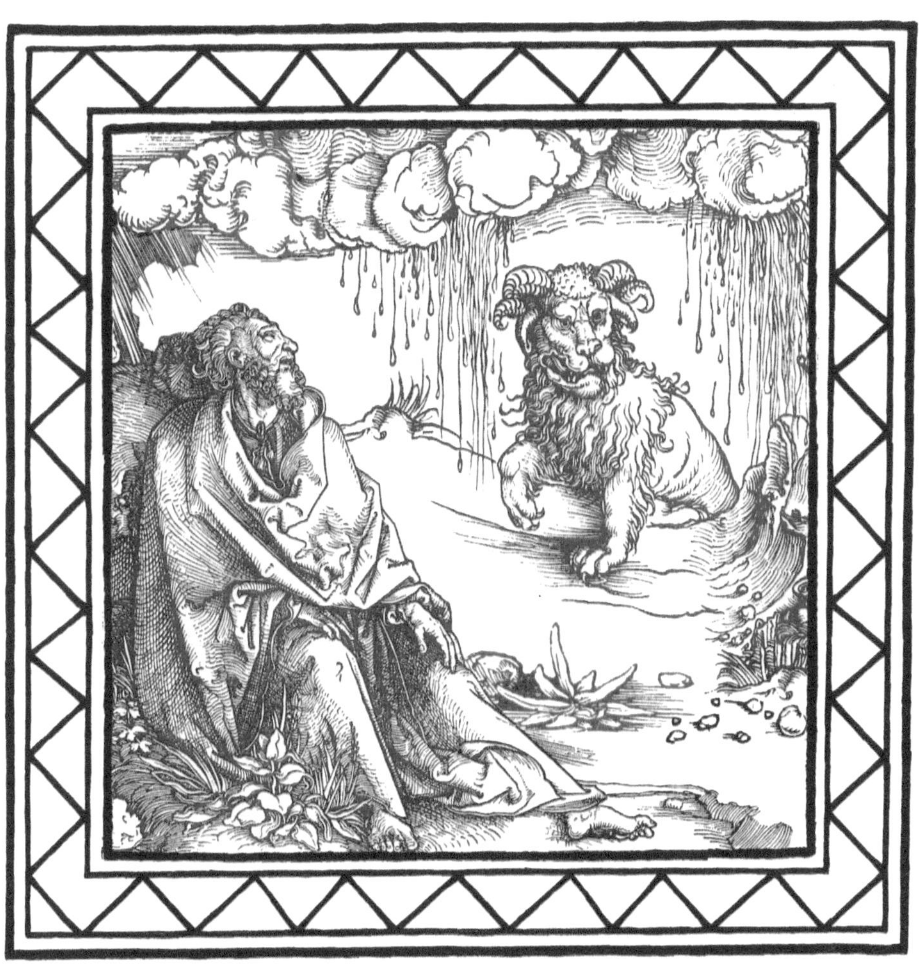

Dreams are explorations of the spiritual world wrapped in a cloth woven from your memories, emotions, and desires.

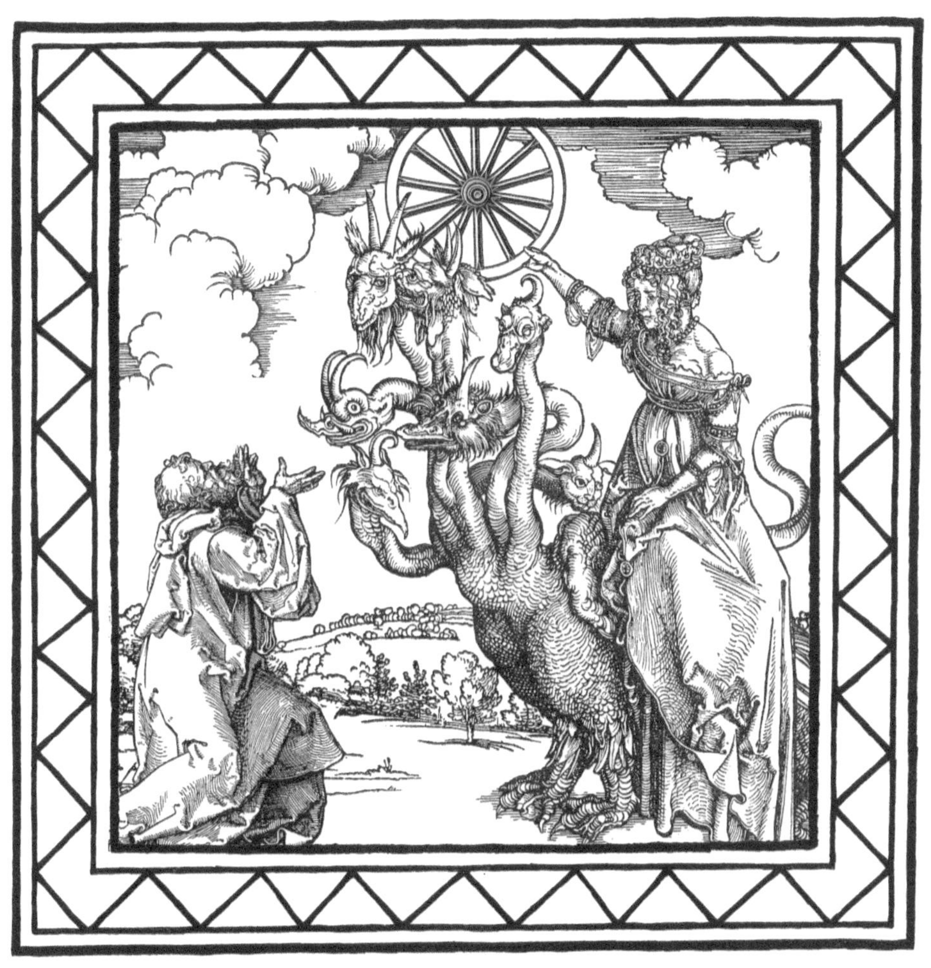

Our minds do not store memories in a literal fashion, but translate our experiences into symbols that are a distillation of a memory, the solidifying of a thought into an iconic shape.

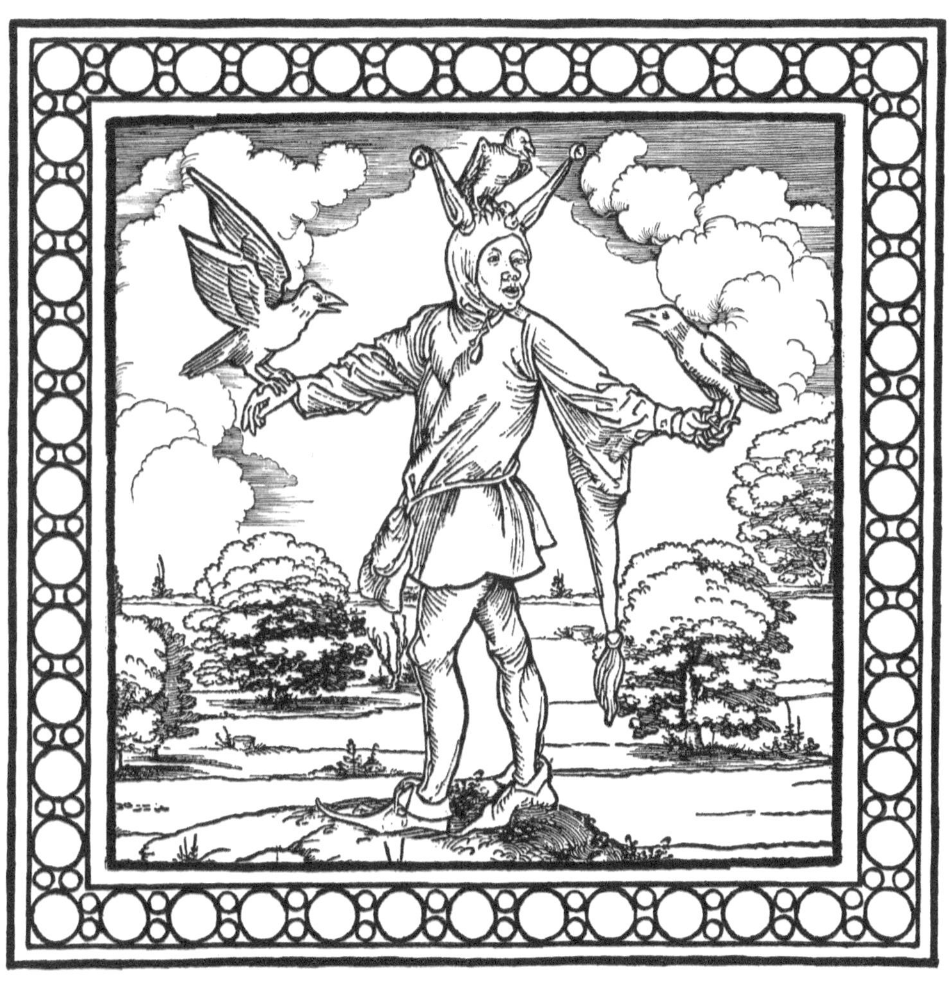

The persons, places, and things in your dreams are called Artifacts. They are remnants, traces, and clues which help us discover and understand the deeper mysteries buried in our souls.

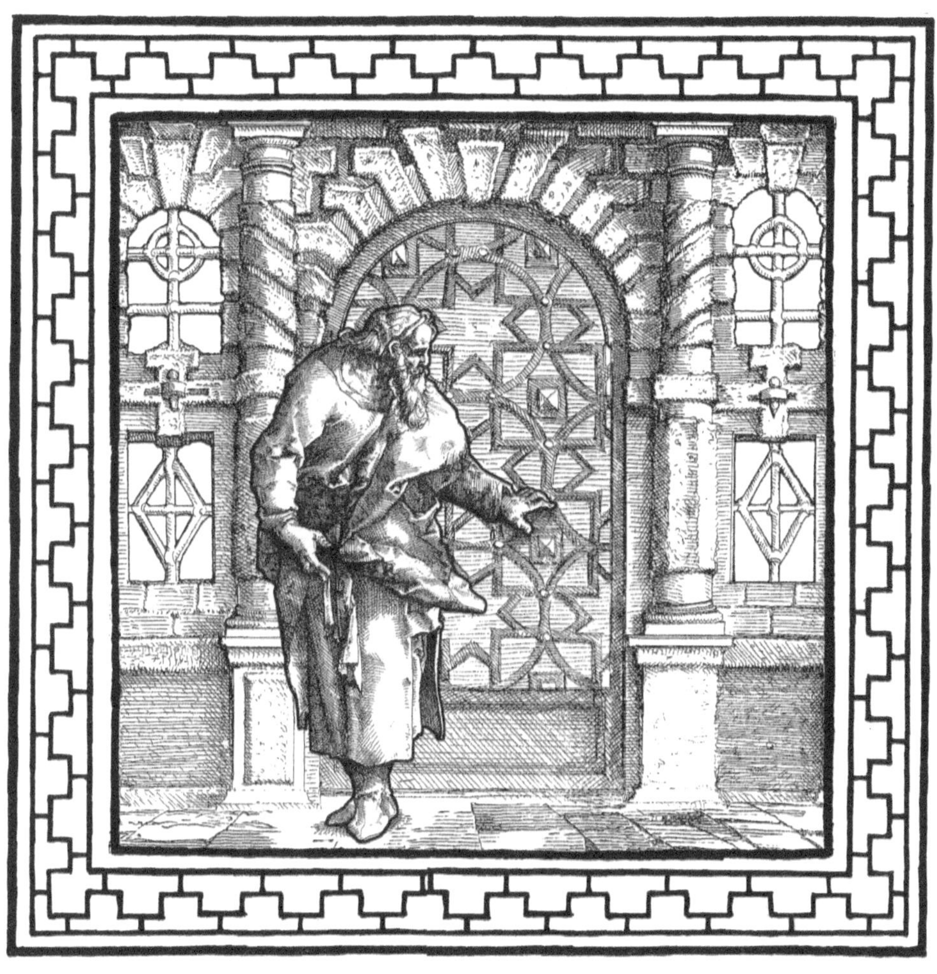

Of all places that exist in your dream world, there is one special place that is the metaphor for your soul. This is called your Dream House.

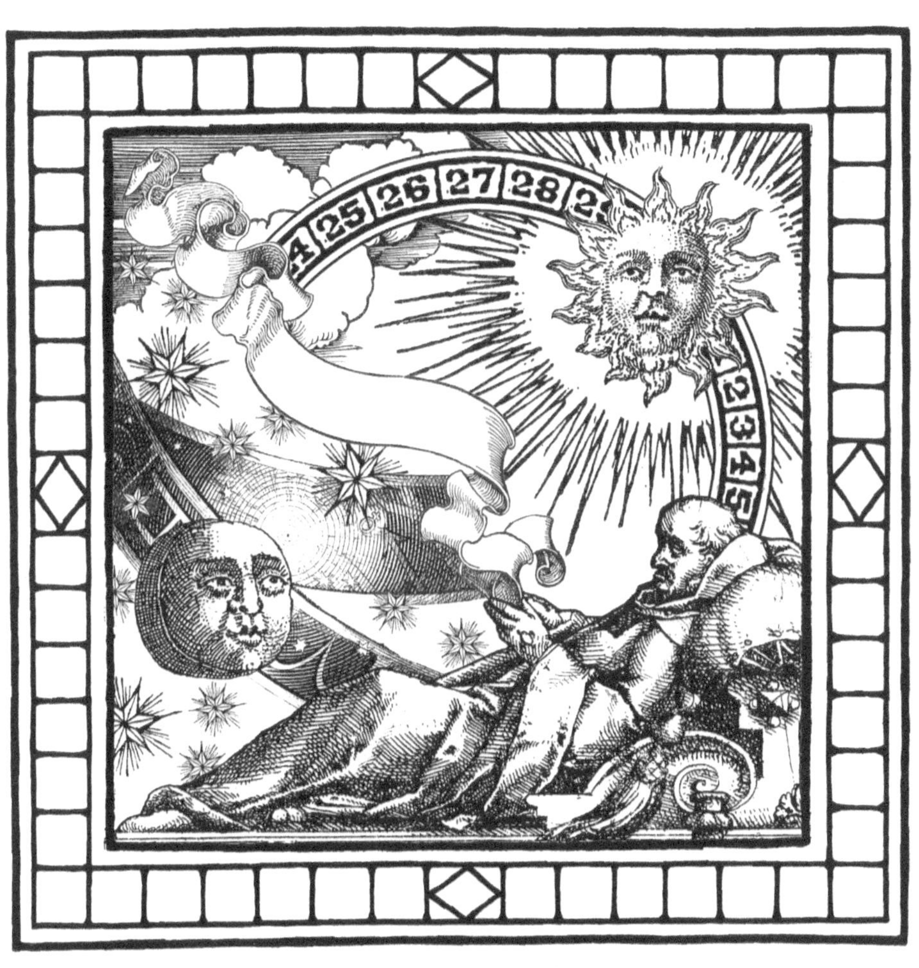

Dreams exist outside of our normal waking time. We may have dreams of things that have happened, are happening now, or may happen in the future.

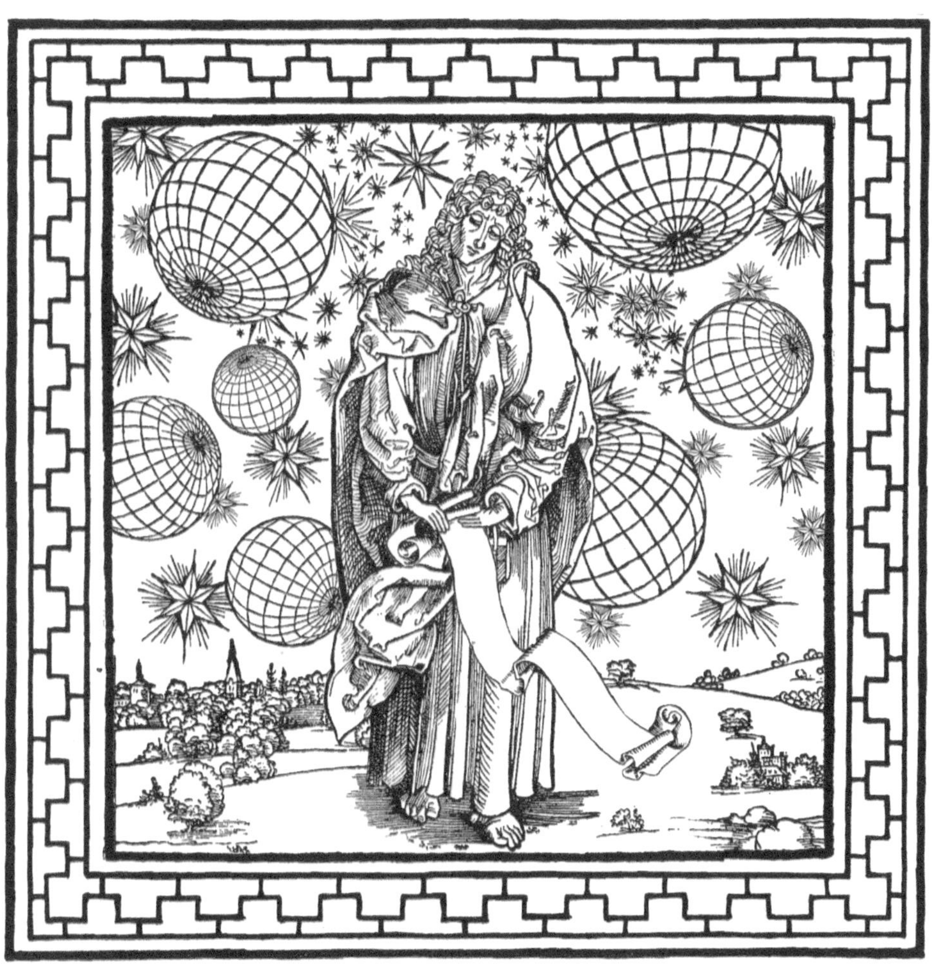

As we learn from our dreams, we build bridges within our divided Self, healing our fractured Soul. All of us are broken in some way, and self-knowledge through our dreams is a wholesome and healing force.

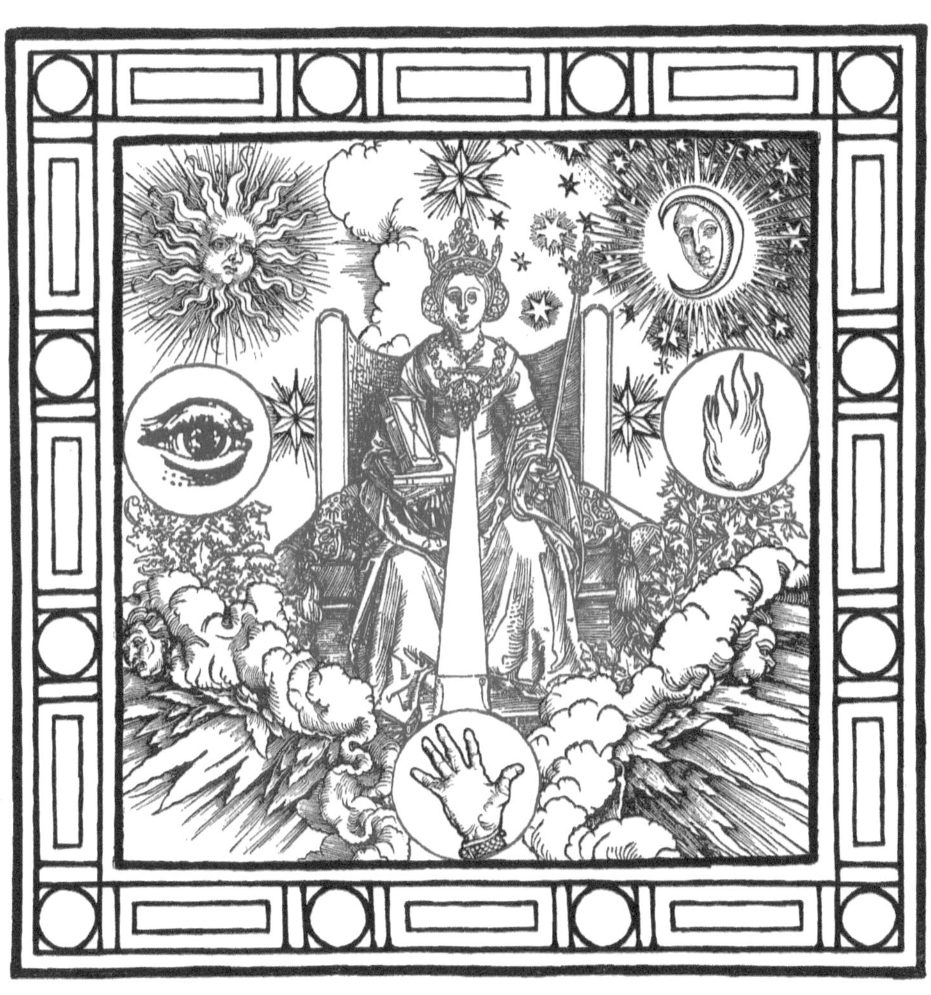

Reflecting creation, our triune nature is composed of three parts: the Body, the Mind, and the Soul. Dreams act as a bridge connecting these aspects of our selves.

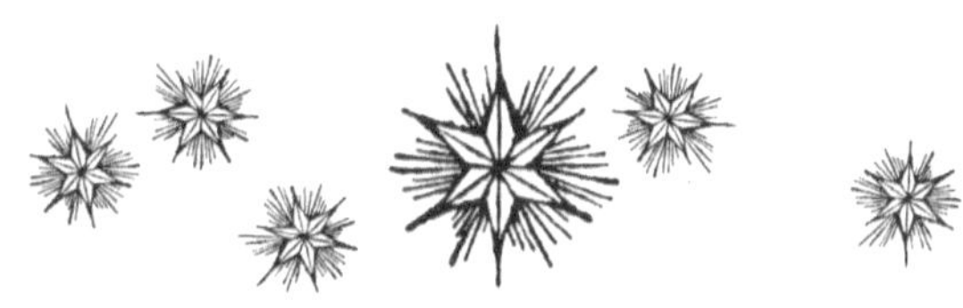

Types of Dreams

II

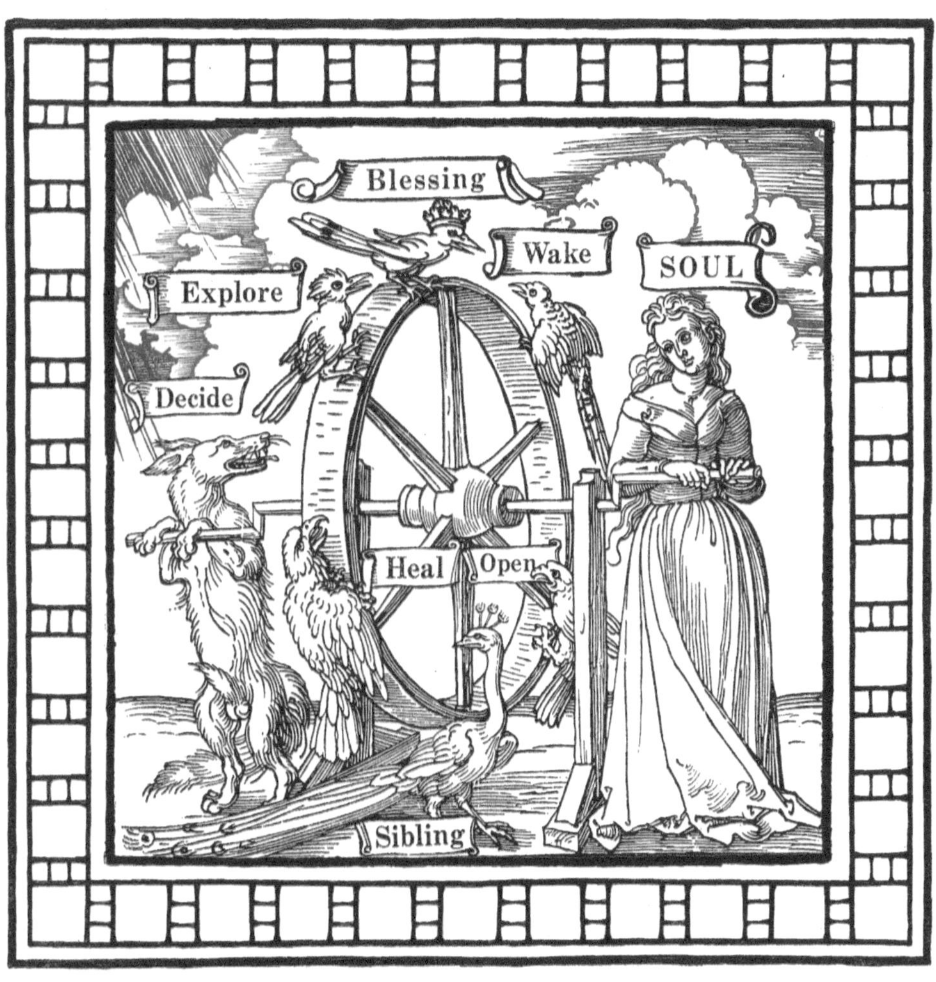

While the spectrum of dreams is wide and diverse, there are only seven principle types. They are Healing, Decision, Puzzle, Exploratory, Sister, Visitation, and Waking Dreams.

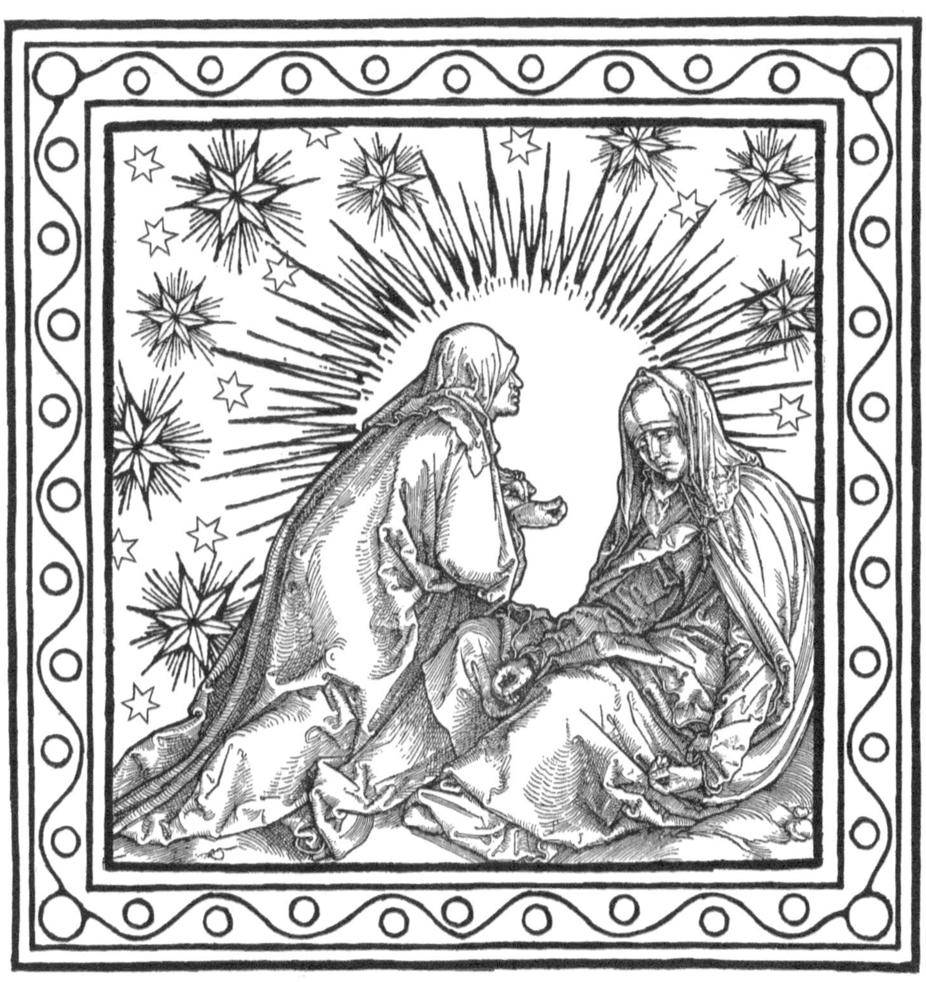

Our bodies speak to us constantly, and Healing Dreams are just one of several languages our bodies use to communicate with our conscious mind.

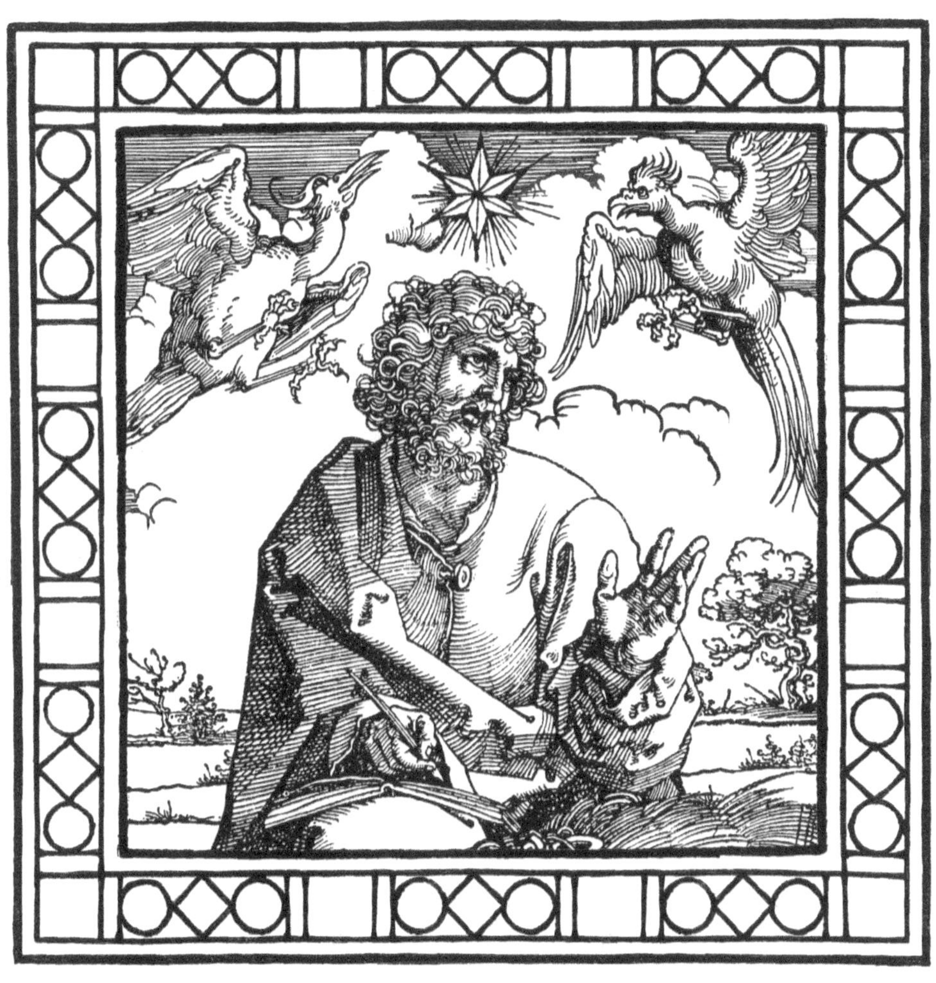

Decision Dreams enable us to make difficult choices by tapping into our deepest memory, emotion, and intellect.

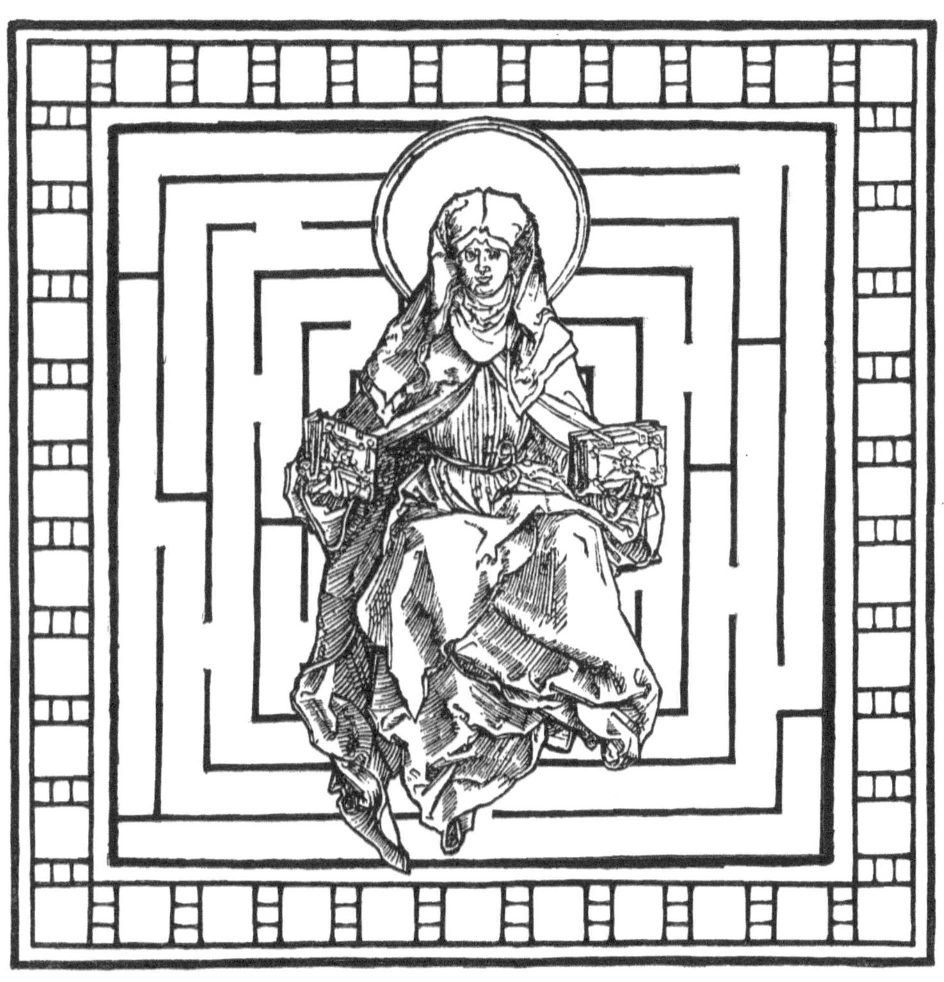

Puzzle Dreams tap into hidden reserves of intuition so that we may approach problems from a new perspective.

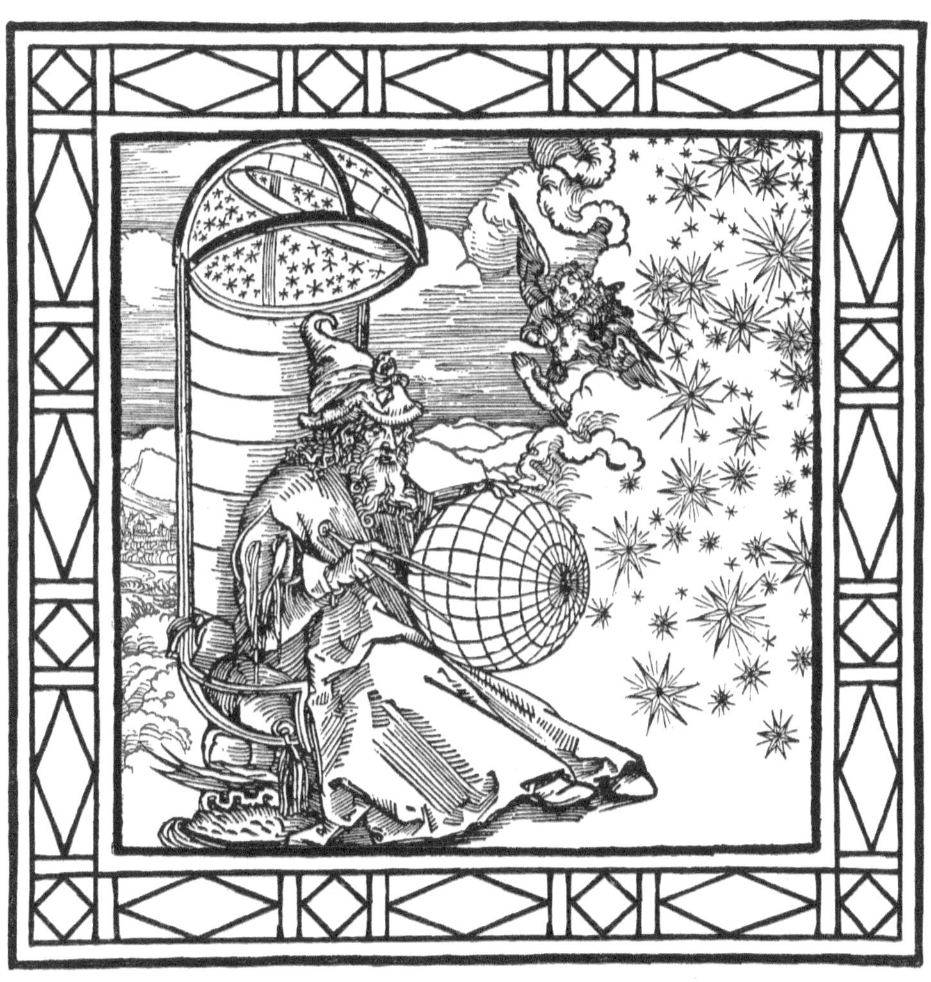

Exploratory Dreams take us on expeditions of self-discovery, returning with trophies of truth and knowledge.

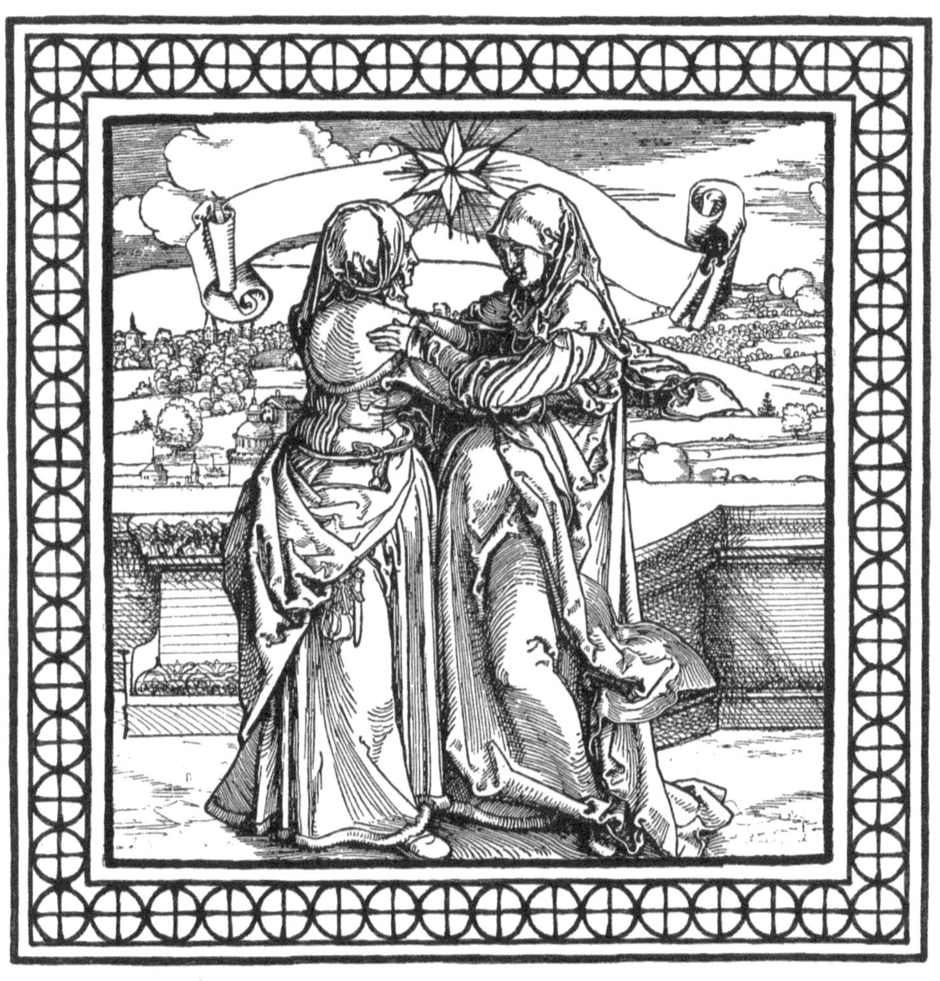

In the fury of an electrical storm, lightning may strike miles apart, but still be from the same storm. Likewise, Sister Dreams may be separated by months or years, but are still products of a single emotional tempest raging across the landscapes of the soul.

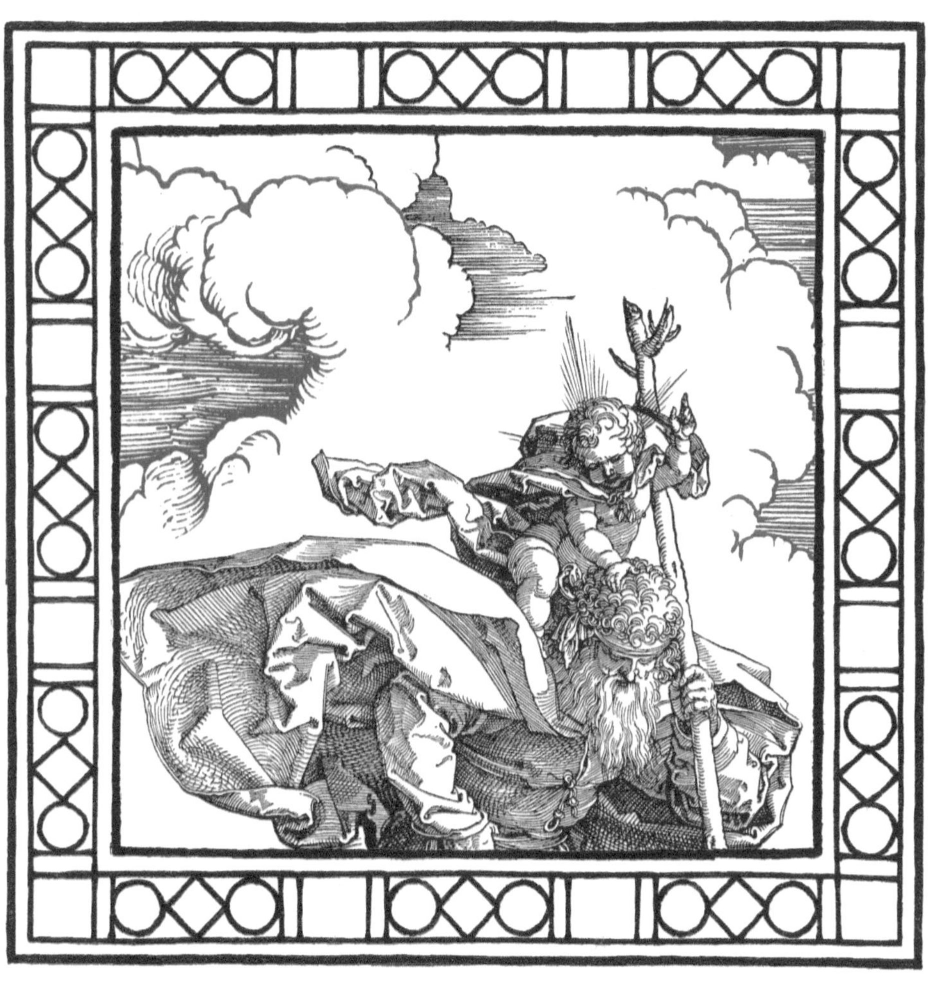

When our Creator reaches out and speaks to us directly, these are Visitation Dreams. These dreams are rare events, and happen only when needed.

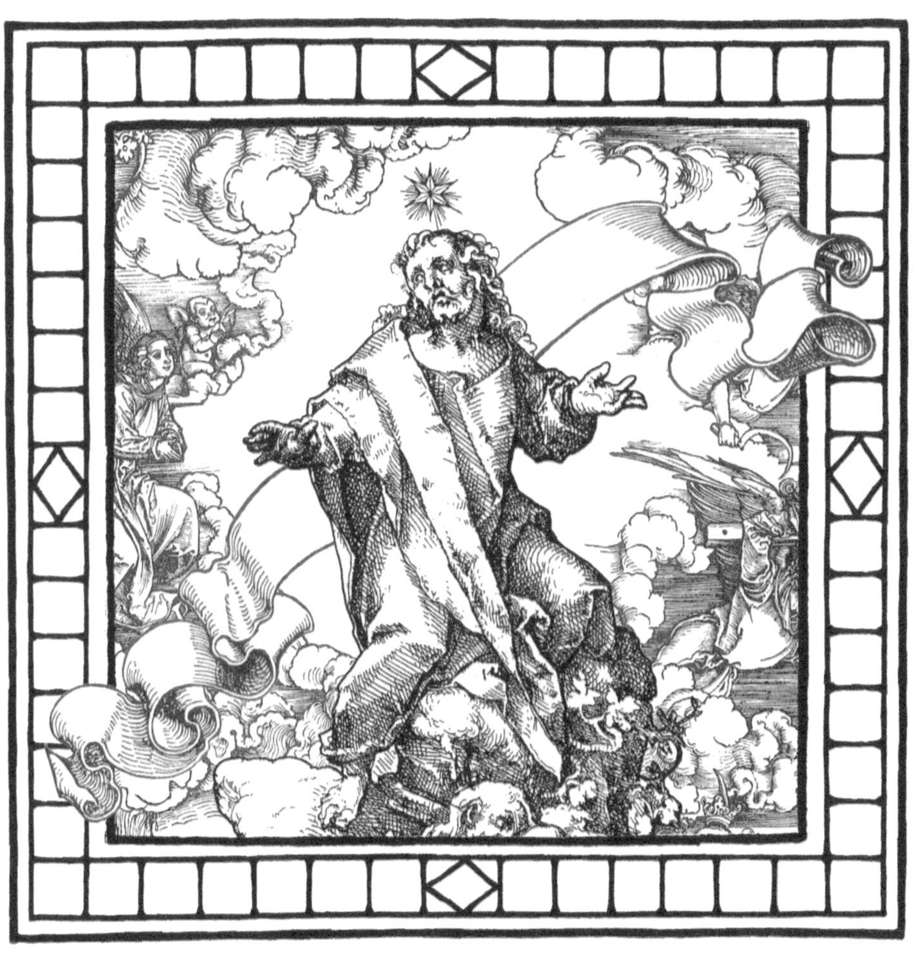

The most important type of dream is called a Waking Dream. This kind of dream represents a higher level of dreaming, a state of consciousness above normal experience.

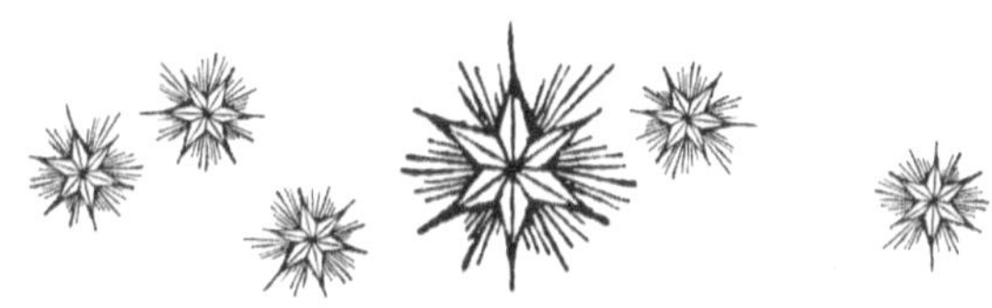

Your Dream Research

III

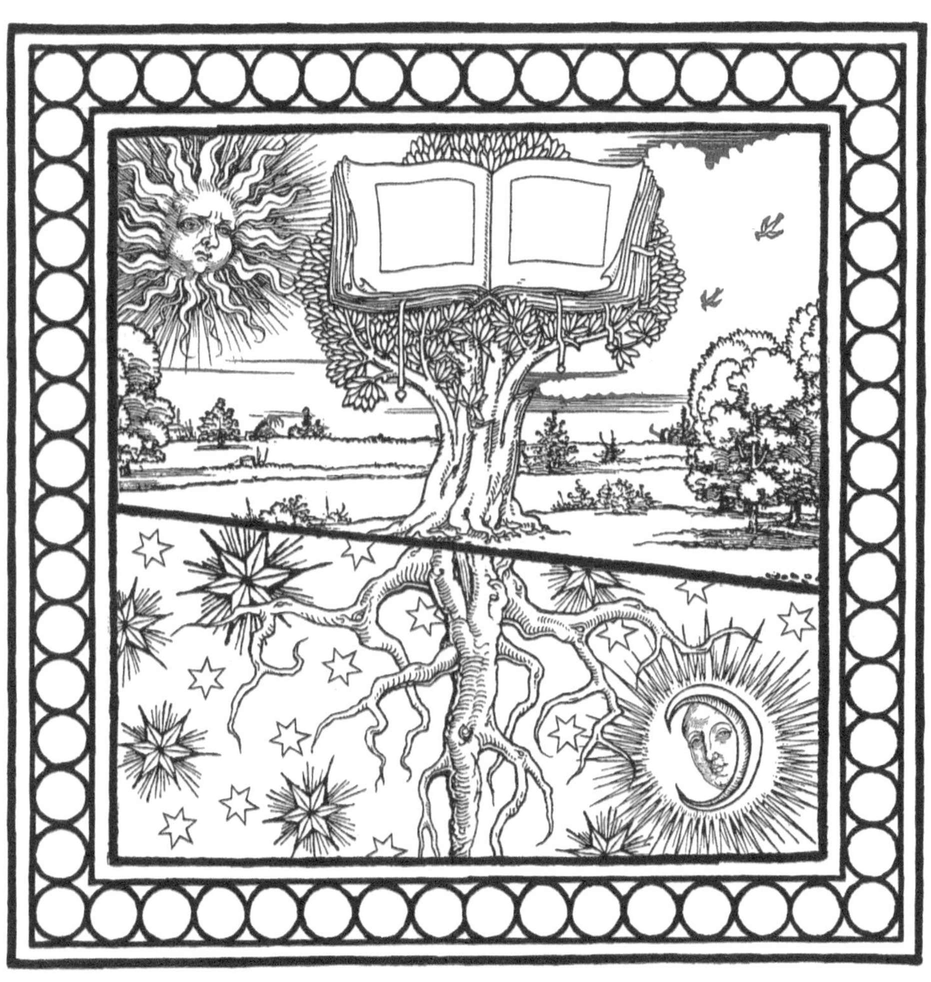

As in all creation, dreams have their own natural rhythms and cycles. Your Dream Tree has seasons of bearing fruit and lying fallow, of blossoming and withering.

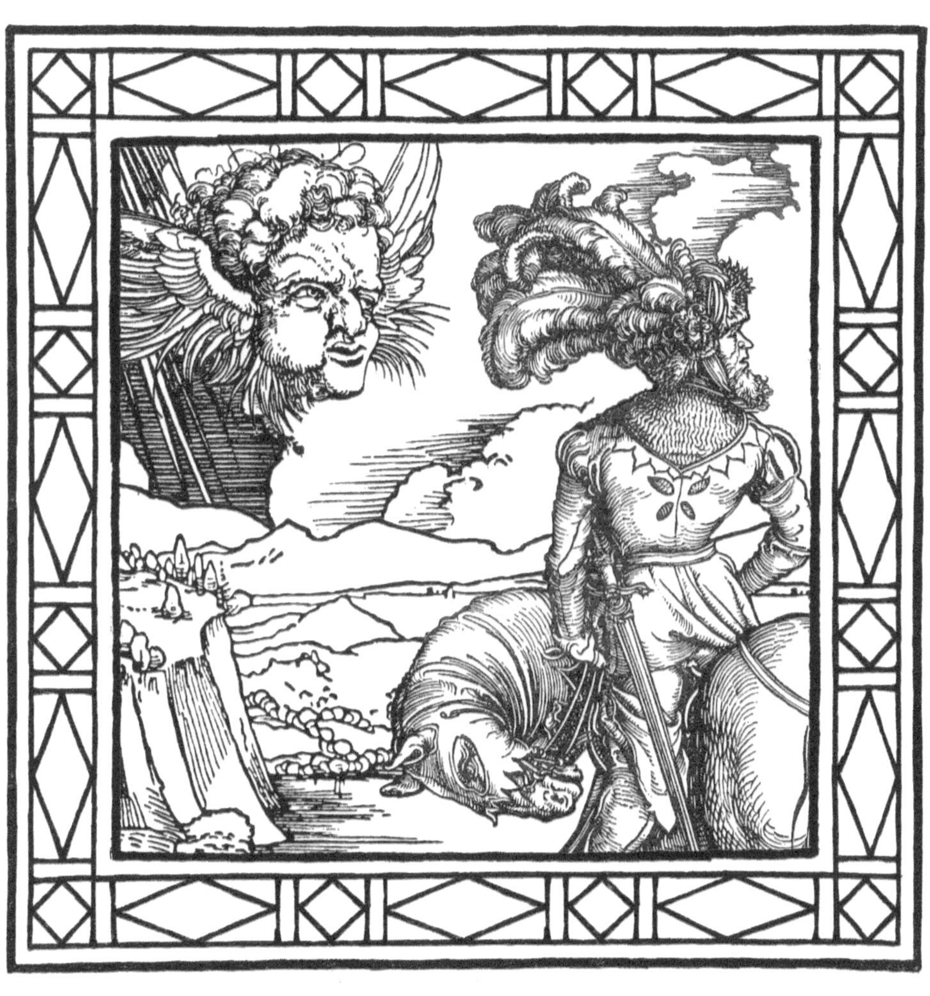

In dreams, we tell ourselves many stories, our Souls teaching our Minds through parables.

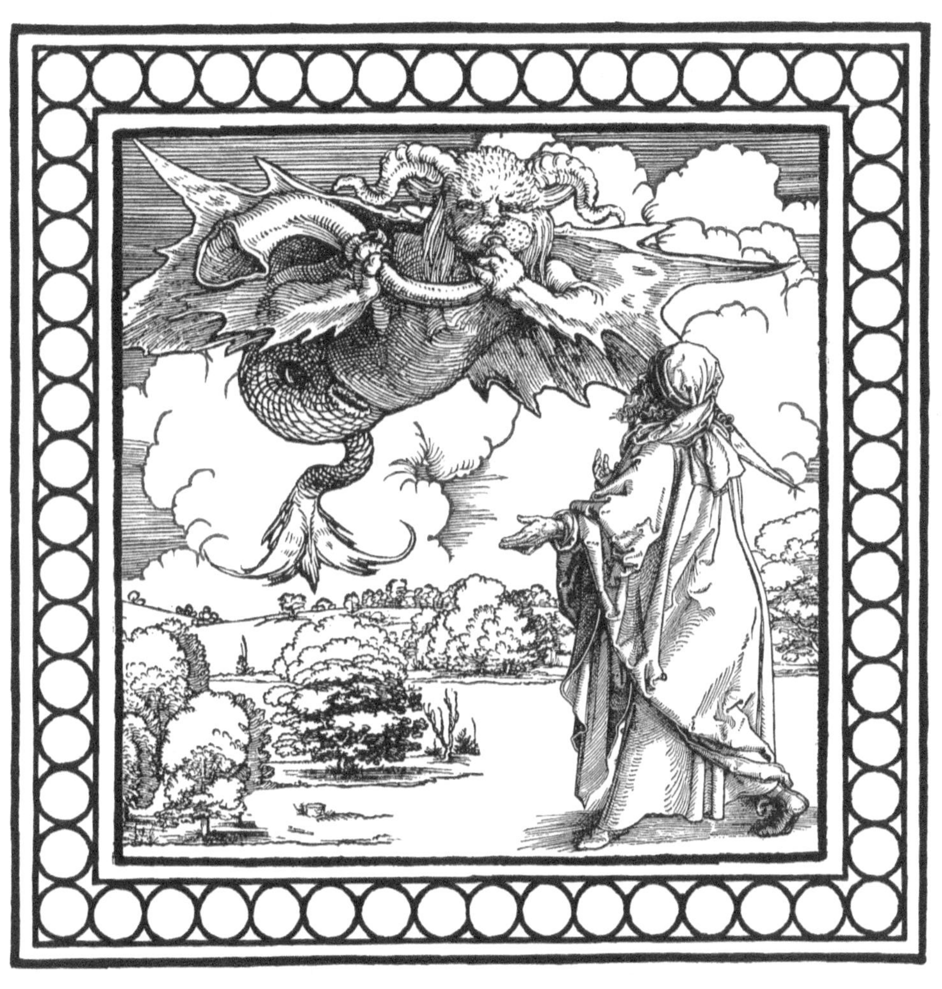

Each person has a different Inner Language, and symbols appearing in your dreams have unique meanings known only to you.

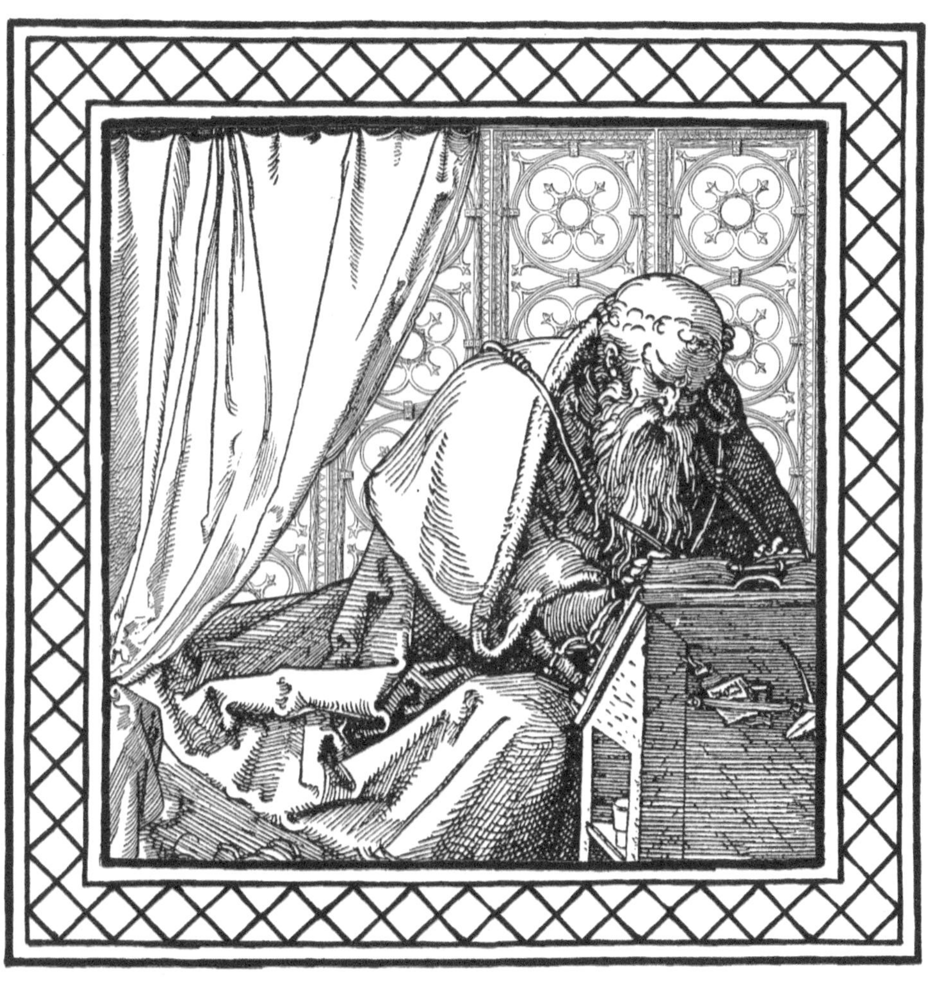

By recording your dreams in a journal, as well as the events in your waking life, a correlation may be established which will help you understand your inner language.

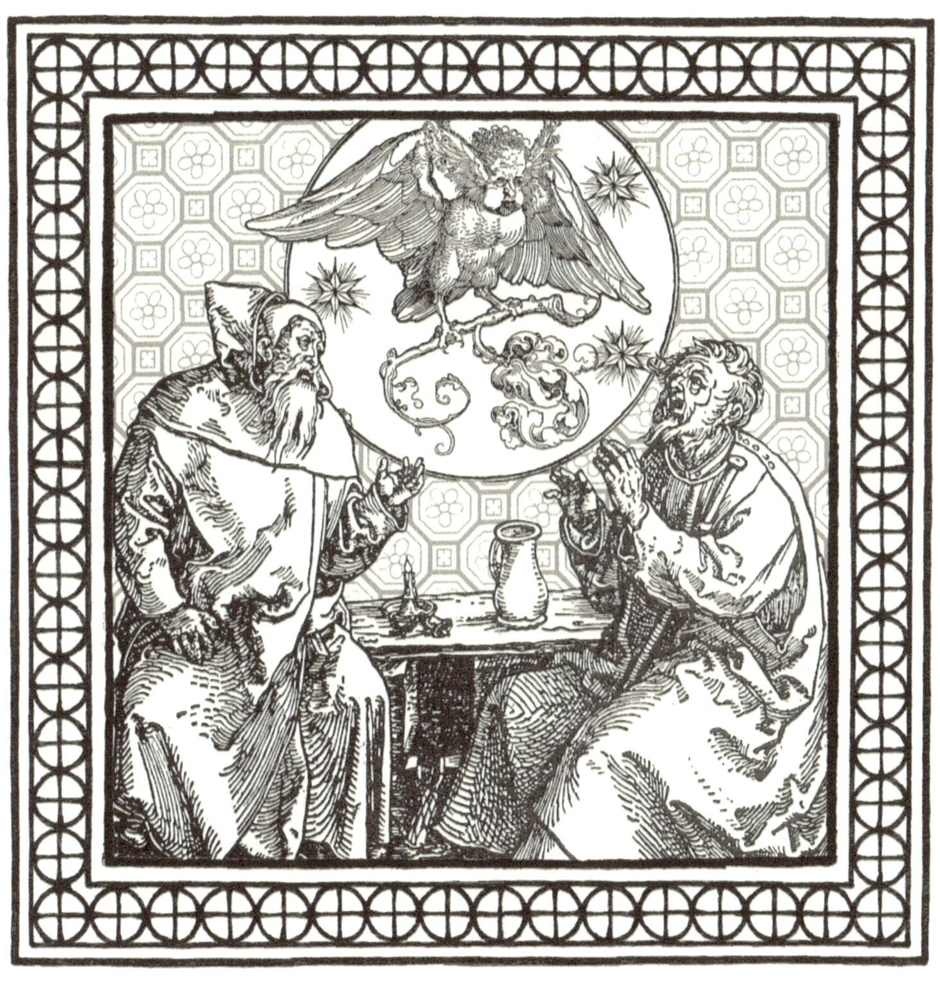

Sharing your dreams is another path to understanding them. The act of speaking brings the dream into the material world, inviting us to view it from a new perspective.

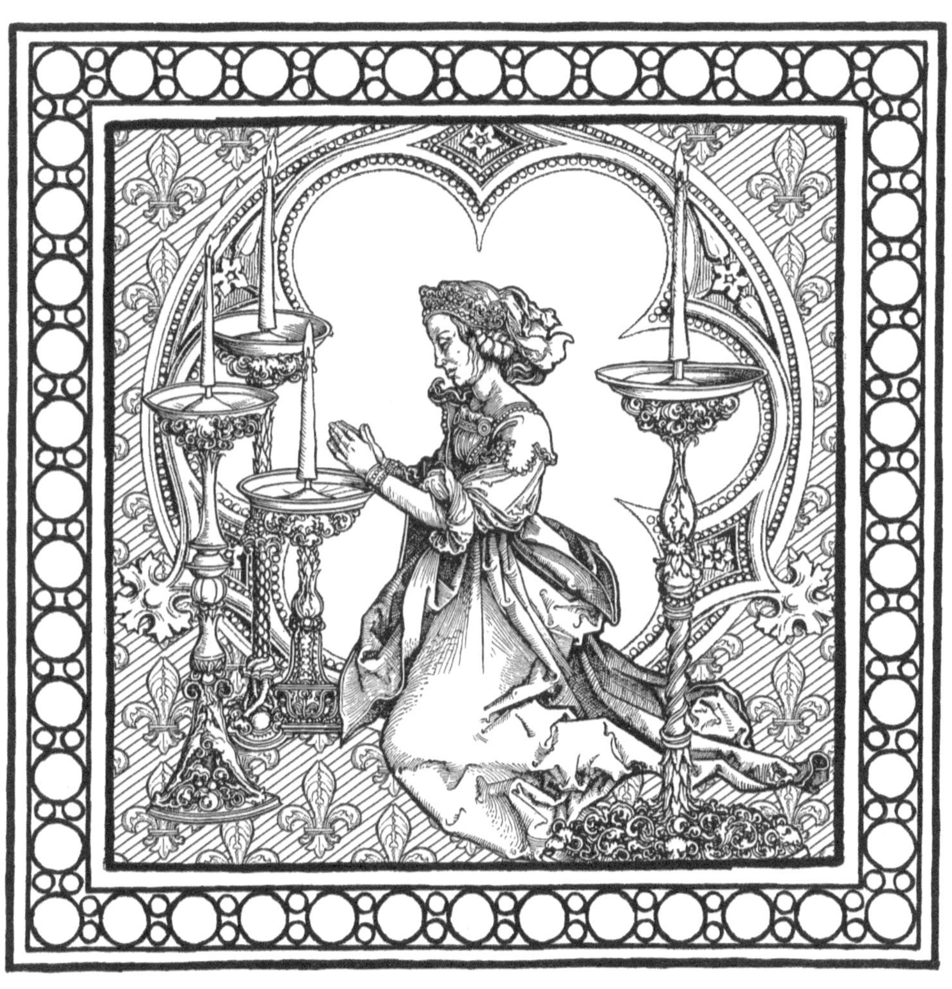

Trusting in the inherent goodness of the Creator, we may seek His help and ask God for dreams of wisdom and guidance.

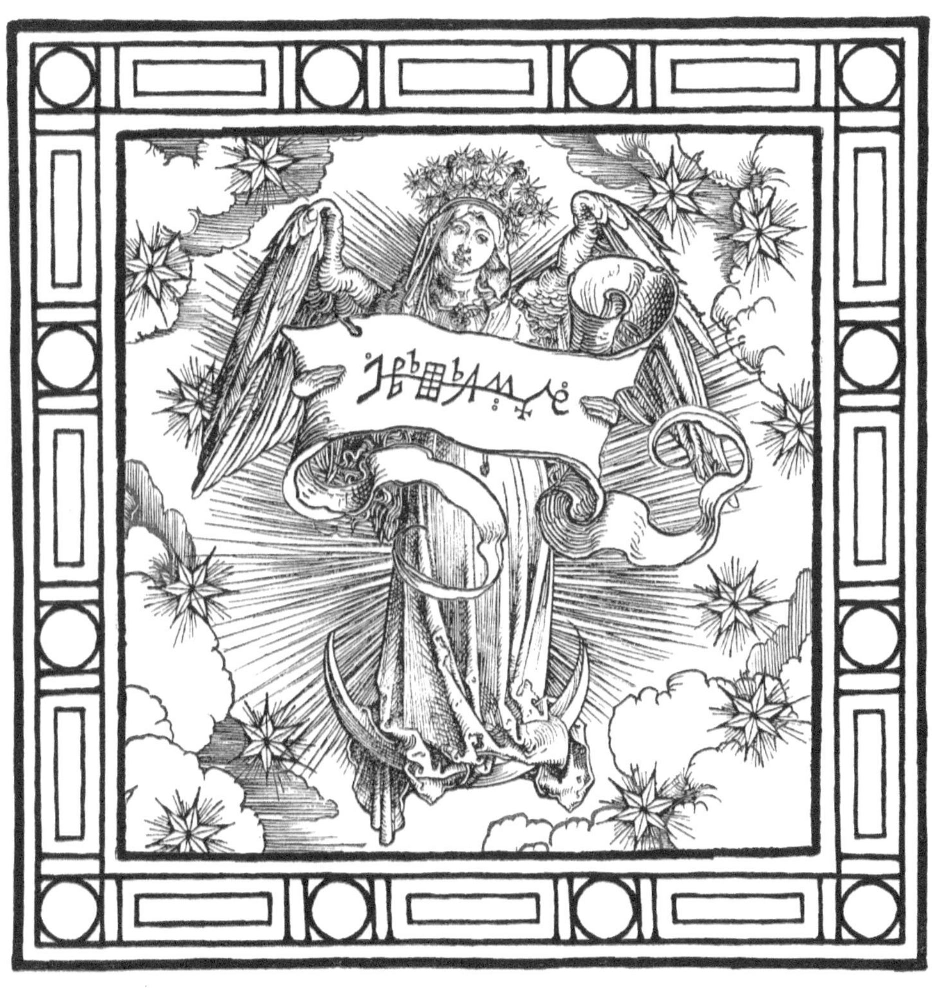

All of Creation yearns to teach us wisdom if we but ask it. The plants, the winds, the sea, and the stars all instruct us in the patterns and cycles of Creation.

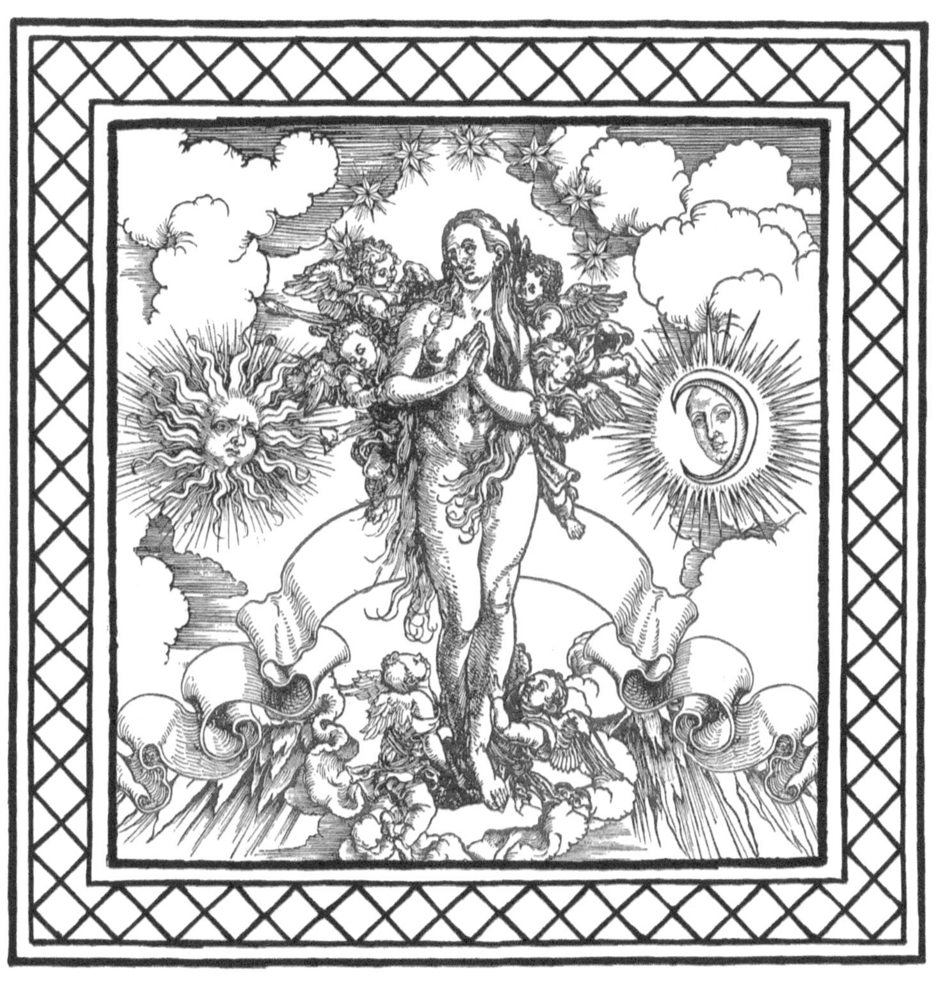

We live within the Dream of God, co-creating the world with our thoughts, words, and deeds. Therefore, dedicate each night's dreaming to Him.

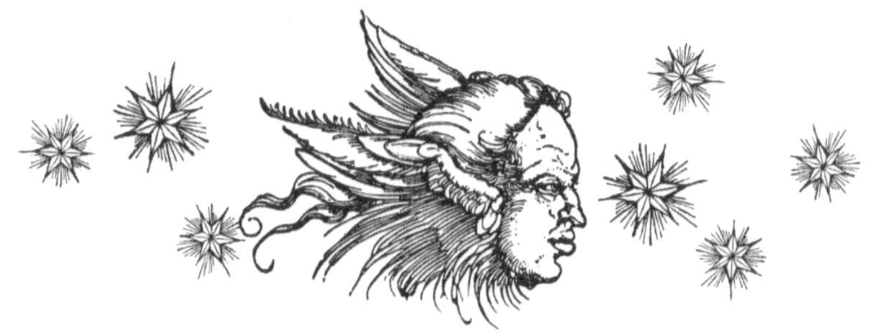

May you dream with love, responsibility, gentleness, and hope, so that the fruit of your dreams will nurture not only yourself, but all of Creation.

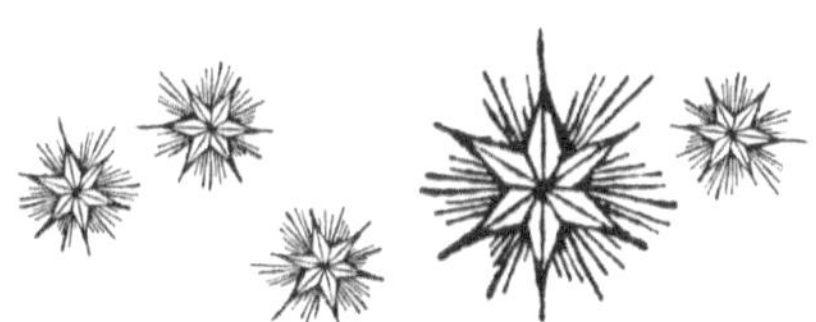

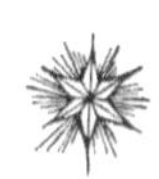

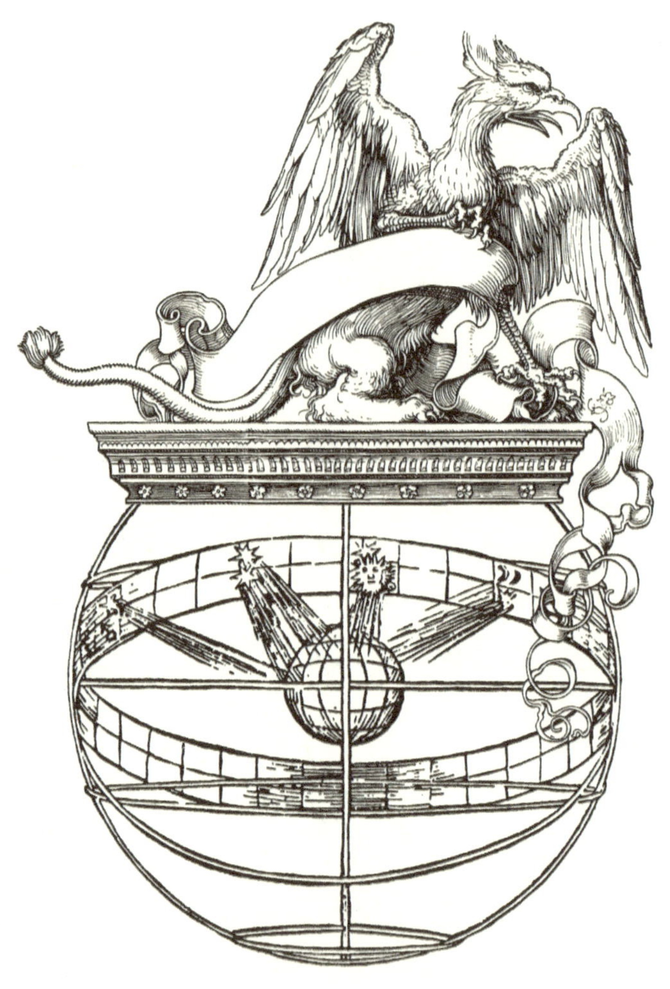

Other Books by Stephen Barnwell

EQUINOX, A Coloring Book

EQUINOX is a coloring book that takes you on a journey into a storybook fantasyland filled with wonder and mystery. Winner of a Bronze Medal in the 2016 Living Now Book Awards.

Oneirognosis, The Art of Dreaming

Learn the Art of Dream Seeding, where you ask your dreams questions and receive answers in return. This book is a meditation on the origins of dreams, the well-spring of creativity, and the interconnection between the mind, body, and soul. It will inspire you to see your dreams from an entirely new perspective. Oneirognosis is the book upon which this coloring book, DREAMTIME, is based.

www.ingramcontent.com/pod-product-compliance
Lightning Source LLC
LaVergne TN
LVHW050944080826
845145LV00004B/1404